SCENES FROM THE PAST:40 (P.

RAILWAY MEMO]
OF
MANCHESTER
AND
STOCKPORT

Stockport Edgeley, 2nd May 1959. Royal Scot Class No **46118** *Royal Welch Fusilier* is seen approaching the platform with the 4.25pm London Road - Birmingham train. Stockport No 2 signal box, seen to the right of the picture, was finally due to disappear after over a century of use as a result of the Manchester South resignalling scheme as the railways moved into the 21st Century. *R.Keeley*

RAYMOND KEELEY

Layout, Design and Typeset by Peter Midwinter
Printed by The Amadeus Press, Cleckheaton.
Published by Foxline Publishing
32 Urwick Rd Romiley Stockport SK6 3JS

London Road Station, 19th August 1959. The 7.58am London Road to Marple leaving platform 3. The engine, Fowler 2-6-4T No **42374**, was an engine which, at the time, I associated with the line through Reddish to Romiley and Marple. The water tank, a vital necessity in the days of steam power, was a familiar shape that displayed itself at the end of some platforms.

R.Keeley

Central Station, 10th October 1958. The Hall Of Memory. Here we have what might be described as the grace of the Midland style. The Compound has the flavour and even the Fowler tank engine could fit within the phrase. No **40907** is piloting Jubilee No **45616** *Malta G C* on the 4.25pm to St Pancras from platform 6. The Fowler 2-6-4T No **42433** is backing onto the 4.28pm Chester Northgate train. *R.Keeley*

RAILWAY MEMORIES & ENCHANTMENT
of
MANCHESTER
and
STOCKPORT

An Introduction.

' Memories and Enchantment' is, I think, a phrase that suitably underlines my thoughts and feelings in the way they have been influenced by that region of the North West known as Greater Manchester. Though in this book, and part two to follow, I am mainly concerned with the south eastern part of the area, with the occasional border crossing into the edge of northern Cheshire and Derbyshire.

It is the 'how and why' in terms of the railways and canals and their association with the surrounding landscape and, to a degree, how this can relate to local industry. An intermingle that I find fascinating, a word that must also be entwined with the meandering idyllic beauty of some of the river ways.

So now a few thoughts about historical and industrial backgrounds, since either or both can become the most interesting feature concerning the appearance and character of many of our towns and cities. Of course it can vary according to area though, be it ancient historical or more recent industrial in terms of background, there is usually a link with the past that is sufficiently strong and clear to allow an easy association with the place name.

In the case of an historical connection it can perhaps stretch back into the dim distant mists of time, possibly covering well over a thousand years or more. Sometimes there is a prominent structural focusing point, a medieval castle, an ancient cathedral or town walls of great age which can make an immediate contact with that distant past. Britain is indeed favoured with so many beautiful towns and cities that have such a relationship.

In contrast to the above, a notable industrial past is more likely to be concerned with the last two and a half centuries,

Piccadilly and Manchester Royal Infirmary, c.1900's. Though this old postcard only shows part of one of the great buildings from Manchester's past, it also displays some interesting transport from that period. The building is part of the frontage of the original MRI. By the mid 19th century, as the MRI expanded, it would dominate the area now known as Piccadilly Gardens and bus station. The Infirmary was opened in 1755, though during the 18th and 19th centuries the buildings were gradually extended and enlarged to meet the growing demands for hospitalisation and treatment, but by the end of the nineteenth century further expansion and modernisation was required. Thus, in 1902, the present site on Oxford Road was established and the new hospital completed in 1908, the old buildings being demolished in 1910. The two open top four wheeled tramcars would have been in operation by 1903. Flat roofed cover for the upper deck began in 1906 for this series of cars.

particularly since the word industry is usually associated with varied forms of productive activity concerning machinery and mechanization, both in the factories and also relating to the varied forms of transport - canal, road and rail, for the movement of the produce.

Therefore if the name Manchester drifts into the minds eye it is likely to be a view of mills and chimneys and an extensive world of industry and commerce, with the construction of the canals and railways being an essential part of such a development. It is an activity that particularly relates to that century of industrial achievement that we call the Victorian Age, a time when a wide and varied growth for the city and surrounding towns and townships gradually evolved, though it was mainly the emergence

and creation of a great and extensive empire of cotton mills around the area that brought the name Manchester to the forefront of the industrial world.

The mills of work one could call them which, along with the scale of canal and railway building in the area, brought long days of backbreaking sweat and toil for those in what might be termed the lower order of working life. Generations now long departed, both male and female, whose bodies gradually became worn out when they were still comparatively young. They certainly played a part in helping to place the name Manchester alongside the nation,s other great cities.

No doubt it was a physically hard life for the working class, both indoors and out. Indeed, for those working outdoors,

Manchester Royal Infirmary, c.1900's. Since there can be no doubt that the Royal Infirmary building must have been one of the most prominent to occupy the central area of Manchester during the 19th century I thought this old postcard view worth including. It is, in effect, an artists impression of the building as it appeared at the turn of the century, a time when the postcard was very much in use. Apart from showing the large area occupied by the hospital, it also manages to convey something of the importance of some of the great warehouse buildings that dominate the background of this picture. The artist has also included the substantial 188 feet high clock tower that dominated the magistrates courts on Minshull Street, seen to the left of the picture.

Both pictures R.Keeley collection

Albert Square, c.1906. What might be described as an impressive frontispiece view, a magnificent building as seen on an old turn of the century postcard. The photograph certainly emphasises the great 281feet 6 inches high clock tower. Indeed, Manchester Town Hall has a quite unique appearance and it is entirely appropriate that it should occupy part of the central area of a great city. Male attire and horse drawn vehicles would suggest a mid Edwardian period. The contrasting appearance of the two tram cars would also imply a 1906/7 date; one of them being an open top double truck bogie car and the other a single truck four wheeled car. Flat roofed cover for these open top double deck four wheeled cars began in November 1906, the balconies remaining open as seen in the photograph.   *R.Keeley collection*

The progressive development of a commercial environment would also mean that other fine buildings were beginning to appear in the city which, in time, would also play their part in helping to create its character. Some of them, built perhaps over a century ago, were mainly to provide various business and leisure facilities for the local population and visitors, many of them still surviving and offering a similar service to those they were originally built for.

Of these fine buildings I will mention just a few favourites and, without doubt, the first to come to mind must be Manchester's splendid Town Hall. This magnificent building has the good fortune to face directly onto the spacious Albert Square which allows a full view of its superb architectural frontage and the imposing 281 feet 6 inches high clock tower. So perhaps we must be thankful to those, probably in council chambers over a century ago; who had some influence in arranging town centre locations. The Hall was designed by Samuel Waterhouse in an ornate Gothic style and, although building commenced in 1868, it would be nine years before it could be viewed in all its glory - 1868 - 1877! It must surely be the city's most prestigious Nineteenth Century building and one of the finest town hall buildings in Britain.

Now I must mention the nearby Midland Hotel particularly for its one time railway association. A late Nineteenth Century building which I consider to be quite impressive, though perhaps not everybody would agree with that point of view. It is certainly ornamental on a grand scale, which is part of its attraction since great buildings display so many beautifully shaped and framed windows. It is my opinion it was all part of what could be described as Midland Style, which invariably brings to mind the phrase 'Grace and Elegance'. Perhaps what could be described as a one time distant colleague nearly 200 miles away, the other end of the line so to speak, could merit a similar description but on an even grander scale, a necessary requirement since no doubt there was a great deal of competition to provide the grandest station buildings by each of those great railways centering on London and an impressive frontispiece would be essential.

In Manchester, the Midland was somewhat restricted in arranging the positioning of its new hotel, therefore the building could perhaps be visualised as a slightly detached frontispiece for the nearby and magnificent 'Hall of Memory' as I see it, sorry, I should perhaps have used that slightly downgrading phrase, train shed! What a pity that complex business arrangements of another age, in terms of space, didn't allow a Hotel and station togetherness which is all part of the charm of St. Pancras!

From a different age and yet displaying an architectural

building and excavation etc., it would be a world dominated by the pick and shovel and wheelbarrow, a time when so much happened in that period of Manchester's industrial life time covering the late Eighteenth and Nineteenth and the beginning of the Twentieth Century. The building of the canal and railway systems alone required long deep cuttings, lengthy embankments and great viaducts and at least one notable aqueduct. This would mean earth moving and repositioning on a vast scale, when the driving thrust and turn of coupling rods was still mainly provided by human arms and legs!

At the same time great buildings connected with the world of business were gradually emerging. Eventually they would play their part in transforming the city into what can now be viewed as a much treasured historical and architectural landmark. Part of this expansion would of course include the quite robust of appearance and yet stylish commercial/ warehouse buildings, some of which still adorn its central area. They may now be in use for different purposes but, when originally built, many of them were a part of that local industry of cotton from what now seems a distant age. Of course most of the great cotton mills themselves were mainly allocated in what were, in those days, the more outer suburban areas and surrounding townships.

Midland Hotel, The Winter Garden, c.1900's. As mentioned in the introduction, the Midland Hotel does, in my opinion, deserve a place in any list of Manchester's great and elegant buildings. Therefore photographs of the building have appeared in many local books including my own book on Stockport Tramways! However, I thought that this rather different illustration relating to the hotel might be of interest. It is an old postcard view that was probably on sale in the early years of this century. It appears to be an artists impression, probably based on a photograph, of what was named The Winter Garden. Perhaps it is just another way of displaying the overall architectural grandeur that applies to the hotel building. Elegance indeed and, of course, it is the word that for me always relates to that wonderful railway.

R.Keeley collection

grandeur to compare with anything that emerged in the Nineteenth Century came the present Manchester Central Library, completed in 1934. The view of the building from every aspect focusing on the curve, which perhaps was an unexpected form of building to emerge in the centre of a city, dominated by large and more angularly built industrial/commercial buildings, all of which helps to further emphasise its Romanesque/Corinthian style and underline its particular grace and beauty. It is indeed the 'curve' which of course abounds throughout the world of nature and, given a chance, never fails to enhance the elegant shape of some man made creations, the great railway viaducts from the past and even the driving wheels of the great favourites of the steam locomotive world for example.

Though I have chosen these three buildings, mainly for the architectural contrast they present, it must be mentioned that just a short stroll around the city centre will bring many more into view, each presenting their own particular style. They are part of the gradual development of the city and have now become a priceless heritage enriching the whole area and for which we must be grateful to those architects of the past who, in the main, relate to the Victorian/Edwardian period.

Fortunately, many of these architectural classics survived the wartime bombing, though some of the warehouse buildings, particularly those on the western side of Piccadilly, did succumb to the fiery inferno. Similar devastation also afflicted other well established landmarks, like the Victorian buildings and hotel which lay between Victoria Street and Deansgate. Fortunately, other nearby landmarks like the Cathedral and Royal Exchange buildings still survive, though both suffered some damage which, thankfully, could be repaired, so they can still capture our attention.

Post-war came other rather different afflictions which, at the time, would be seen as town centre improvements when, in the 1960's period, the squared and towering blocks of concrete, both for business and housing, began to appear. Convenient for business premises they may have been, but to me they appear quite crude

and without any kind of finesse, architecture wise, especially when compared to an older world of grace and beauty, upon which they often intrude.

However, Manchester was not alone, other towns and cities suffered in a similar way in what has been described as the tower block period, but one's spirits begin to rise when journeying around the Manchester area of today and you notice some very significant changes. At first it seemed beyond belief, then you realise that you are witnessing a gradual return to an older world of elegance, both in housing and commercial building development of more recent times.

Apart from some fine city centre buildings, the suburbs and surrounding towns and townships can also present the viewer with some quite large and impressive buildings, many of which were once stalwarts of the kingdom of cotton. Of the survivors, now in rather different use as business premises, it is the grandeur and robust appearance of the main structures that capture the eye, a basic reason for them to become the focal point of a locality.

Perhaps it is worth mentioning just a couple of examples in the district of Reddish which are very familiar to me. They are quite prominent landmarks that can be clearly seen even from nearby hillsides like Werneth Low. The first consists of the remaining half of the once spectacular Broadstone Mill buildings, the central area of which were once graced by elegant twin chimneys - now demolished. Then, quite nearby and fortunately more or less visually intact where it concerns the main buildings, is the magnificent Houldsworth Mill plus its quite statuesque chimney. This splendid and extensive building, plus some other fine local community buildings nearby with which it is associated, are part of the heritage bequeathed to the area by Sir William Houldsworth, a great businessman and local benefactor who did so much for his Victorian period workforce.

Now moving on beyond the suburbs, one becomes aware that the City of Manchester carries an additional and distinctive honour, for it can clearly be recognised as the pivotal point of a

Fallowfield Station, c.1905. This postcard from the past identifies the view as Fallowfield station, though only part of the station building can be seen on the right hand side of the photograph. Nevertheless the postcard is most interesting, especially concerning the variety of traffic on view. The open top tramcar No **582** was built in 1904 thus it would only recently have been in operation when the photograph was taken. The various horse drawn vehicles are also of interest and in particular the one that appears to be a private horse carriage with a lady waiting to board it. Perhaps she had just arrived at the station and lived in one of the nearby very large houses. The stout brick wall seen on the left hand side of the photograph is from the parapet of the overbridge crossing the railway, both the main lines and the one leading to the goods sidings. *R.Keeley collection*

large area now referred to as Greater Manchester. An honour indeed, for this includes an impressive outer circle of towns and townships which, without doubt, are all important in their own right. The origins of their success in the world of textile and associated industry which, for example, included coal mining, brick manufacture etc., all of which would influence the gradual development of the areas railway systems in the Nineteenth Century, with the resulting growth of railway memorabilia. Sadly though, so much of the latter, especially in terms of buildings and the 'ways', are now no more than visions in the minds eye, or more visual contributions from the cameras eye!

Without exception, each of these towns and townships possess their own individual character and style, part of which can sometimes be related to the surrounding landscape, more especially when a river valley forms a central point - power for the mills etc.! For the visitor, there are also a variety of majestic town hall buildings to be viewed - the stately and magnificent examples at Stockport and Bolton immediately come into mind.

I must also mention the areas good fortune in its possession of some ornate market halls. One example, only recently built, makes a stylish addition to the buildings in the town centre of Wigan, its ornamental clock tower clearly indicating a return to an older and more gracious form of architecture. There are other market halls in the locality that date back to a distant past and a quite different world, but they remain a much loved and graceful adornment to a town and are usually well cared for and well used by the local population. Personally, I have a particular affection for the splendid halls in Stockport and Ashton. Once inside either of these buildings you can become captured by the atmosphere, an overall friendly peace and tranquillity, below which is the quiet bustle and conversation of local people which, thankfully, is usually undisturbed by raucous music - *noisac* as I usually describe it!

For the rail enthusiast and other people interested in the architecture of the area, Greater Manchester once provided a variety of interesting station buildings, both of local and mainline importance, but many of them have now disappeared, though

ironically, railway buildings sometimes remain long after the railway has been abandoned and its permanent (cynical word!) way removed. I am thinking particularly of two examples in the Greater Manchester area where the station booking offices fronted onto a main road with steps down to the appropriate platforms. In effect these buildings form a facade on a road where the latter crosses the ghostly cutting of a railway. Ghostly, well yes, because it is now minus the rails and has been minus local passenger services for many decades. These buildings may now provide for different business or other facilities, but their original and graceful structural character remains intact, for which we can be thankful.

Fallowfield and Levenshulme South are the two examples that I have in mind since they are now endowed with what could be described as a form of preservation. In either case I can stand somewhere nearby viewing what is now a barren trough of despair and then allow my imagination to run riot. Far below I can hear the almost underground rumble of a 'Sandringham' or 'Director' pounding along to Sheffield and Marylebone. Ghostly visions maybe, but the memories are still there.

Awaiting those with a desire for further exploration, there are the long abandoned, but still visible - though now grass grown, ways. Idyllic views from overbridges or otherwise, all contributing to the nostalgia which, in turn, creates a feeling of sadness for opportunities lost. Futility is the word that comes to mind.

In some areas, the 'ways' are becoming gradually more concealed either by the ceaseless activity of nature, which is at least benign, or the harsher activity of cuttings filled in with earth and rubble. The latter seems almost to underline pangs of conscience at the wasteful casting aside of something that could still be of use in todays world. Modern tramway development perhaps? Well, it's a thought in these days of traffic crush and crisis. Never mind, just fill it in and forget it. I suppose that is the short sighted view to take, especially if the imagination can perhaps only conjure up a rather limited and blinkered vision of future needs and possibilities

However, enough of my cynicism, I must get on with my journeying, by rail of course, **........ continued on page 10**

Manchester Central, 10th October 1958. "Some might consider me to be just an old goods locomotive, but here I am on the 4.03pm Manchester Central - Sheffield Midland!" This train stopped at all stations and ran via Stockport Tiviot Dale, Romiley, Marple, New Mills to Chinley, then along what I can only ever think off as the Hope Valley Line, with its superb views of hillsides and valley. The line has variable gradients but these large Fowler 0-6-0's could cope with them quite well. After all, they had a tractive power that could compare with many of the passenger locomotives around at the time, 4-4-0's and 4-6-0's. In 1958 No **44547** was based at Sheffield Grimesthorpe, as indicated by the shed plate 41B on the smokebox door. No **40907** was a nearby colleague at 41C Millhouses. No **44547** was basically of Midland design though improved by Fowler and was built at Crewe in 1928.   *R.Keeley*

Manchester Central, 5th April 1957. The grace and elegance of the Midland Compounds can be clearly observed from whatever angle one chooses and on that day I did photograph No **41118** from several positions before travelling behind her to Stockport Tiviot Dale. Though built in early LMS days, 1925, it has to be a 'Midland' Compound since in those early days Derby still had considerable influence on locomotive design policy. After taking the photographs and before boarding the train I had a word with the driver, a very friendly man. He told me that the engine was only recently ex works after a major overhaul, the gleaming paintwork being a form of evidence. He thought she had survived because of the soundness of the frames. Even so, the locomotive didn't have long to go before being withdrawn in January 1958.   *R.Keeley*

Near Fallowfield Station, October 1947. Not a very good photograph in terms of print quality, it was taken shortly after my return home from demobilization. I was using a "box" Brownie camera which I had bought while stationed in Egypt prior to my journey back to England. However, the location is interesting. The local train had just left Fallowfield station and passed under Ladybarn Lane bridge, the engine being LNER Class B9 No **6109**, one of those robust locomotives designed by J.G.Robinson. The cutting through which it is riding along still exists but now a trough of memory and sadness for years of lost opportunities.   *R.Keeley*

(Centre) Fallowfield Station, May 1974. A platform view of the main buildings of Fallowfield station as they appeared in May 1974. The station had closed for passenger services in July 1958 though a single line, the Up line, would remain for another sixteen years. This would mainly be for use as an occasional east - west through route for some freight traffic. It always seems to me like a form of contradiction when a station may lose its fine buildings though its passenger services remain in use. Then we can discover the complete opposite, station buildings remaining in use for a veriety of reasons and perhaps long after passenger facilities and indeed the whole of the rail track has long disappeared.   *R.Keeley*

(Bottom) Levenshulme Station, October 1975. A rear view of the station as it appeared in 1975. The part of the Up platform in the view appears quite solid though the Down platform seems to be crumbling away. In both cases nature has grasped the opportunity of 17 years they have been unused. The stairway to the Down platform can still be observed, though it appears solidly blocked, while that leading to the Up platform has been removed. The main building, with the rather ornate little dome like addition to its roof, fronts on to the main road, the A6. Since the line was closed it has been used for providing other business facilities for the public. Beyond the overbridge, carrying the weight of the buildings and main road, another bridge can just be seen. This carries the main line between Stockport and Piccadilly, both of which are crossing what I have described elswhere as a 'trough of despair'.   *R.Keeley*

London Road Station Manchester

continued from page 7........ though occasionally using the walking legs that nature provided! This time it is to the south and east of the area with minor crossing of county boundaries en route where, as will be revealed in due course, it is the intermingle of rail, rivers, canal and surrounding landscape and their historical content and connection that forever continues to captivate me.

Of course the rivers and valleys are, in a manner of speaking, quite timeless. Therefore, the man made 'ways' of the past were forced to accept and conform, to some degree, with the twists and turns required by the world of nature. Indeed the 'how and why' of this circumnavigation is always fascinating to observe and some aspects of this will become even more apparent in part two.

Initially however our journey begins at a great railway station whose long lived interior became a vast chamber for so many of those great voices of the steam locomotive world, from base to baritone and tenor. Therefore the sheer atmosphere of this great glass enclosed space can do much to enrich those of us with memories and imagination for the past, the enchanting and ghostly sounds from another age, all part of the wonder of the minds eye and ears, so to speak.

So we must be grateful that the original interior of the station is still with us, even though it is now deprived of its one time stylish facade, which could be described as its Victorian *Top Hat, Top Hat and Tails* being a phrase that, ... *continued on page 15*

The Edwardian Age, c.1904/5. An old postcard that probably dates from around 1904/5. Interesting in that not only does it show two notable buildings with the cathedral tower being the most prominent, but, as on the post card of the old infirmary, it also displays some vintage tramcars. The building hovering in the left background being the rather Italianate front of Exchange station. Sadly, this was destroyed in the 1940 Manchester blitz. Of the tramcars, No **161** was a four wheeled open top car and No **447** an open top bogie car. Both were built in the 1901/02 period.
    R.Keeley collection

Just a Random Thought.

Since the name Exchange has found its way into the caption for a previous photograph, I thought it would provide an opportunity to recall its nearby and close companion with the famous name, Victoria, especially as both stations, along with Central and London Road are part of a foursome that helped to establish Manchester's railway heritage. It relates to a great and distinguished century. Each of them has suffered forms of structural damage and change, which, to some degree might be considered by rail enthusiasts as part of a lost world. Therefore, although this book is mainly concerned with railways in a different area of Greater Manchester, I thought that one or two photographs of Exchange and Victoria might be worthwhile, more especially those internal views displaying the exhilarating power of steam.

Exchange Station, 20th May 1960. Two stalwarts of the Stanier age, both appearing anxious to take full view! At platform 1, Class 5 No **45372** has just started to move out on the 5.07pm Exchange to Chester via Newton le Willows. Jubilee Class No **45634** *Trinidad* will follow shortly afterwards from platform 2 with the 5.10pm to Windermere, the shedplate number 5A denotes it as being from Crewe.   *R.Keeley*

Exchange Station, 15th January 1958. A massive flurry of steam exhaust as Royal Scot Class No **46156** *The South Wales Borderer* emerges from under the overall roof of Exchange with the 10.05am Newcastle - Liverpool Exchange - 3.23pm Victoria. The shed plate number on the smoke box door is 8A (Edge Hill). The graceful arched roof was obviously undergoing extensive structural repairs, the time of the year being apparent by the slight scattering of snow.   *R.Keeley*

Exchange Station, 15 January 1958. Though built at Derby Works in 1930, Class 2P No **40631** is still, at least to me, a Midland 'Simple' with a shadow of Deeley hovering in the background! The engine has just had a refill of that essential liquid without which the natural world, human and otherwise, could not survive, all part of the fascinating life of these creatures built of steel. The circular water tank and supply columns are positioned at the east end of platform 2. In the early days of steam, the water columns could be seen in convenietly located positions at many of our larger stations, quite apart from the loco sheds. In 1959 No **40631** was shedded at 26F, (Patricroft). *R.Keeley*

Victoria Station, 19th May 1972. A view taken from Hunts Bank, which shows part of the lengthy new station building designed by William Dawes and completed in 1909. One could see it as a fine and appropriate piece of architecture, a celebration for the final extension of the station that was carried out in the earlier part of the century. My own photograph combines a form of ancient and modern, though the original name of the railway and the evergreen name of the station is clear to observe! *R.Keeley*

Victoria Station, 9th May 1959. Jubilee Class No **45698** *Mars* leaving platform 12 with the 11.28am train to Newcastle. The train will be taking the Loop line, which can be seen curving away just beyond the Victoria East signal box, then onward to Thorpes Bridge Junction with Rochdale the next stop. ***R.Keeley***

Victoria Station, 27th December 1957. Jubilee Class No **45708** *Resolution* on the 11.00am Liverpool Lime Street - Hull, 11.58 from Manchester Exchange. The engine is bracing itself for the mile long steep gradient, (between 1 in 47 and 1in 59), up to Miles Platting. A banking engine at the rear of the train would have been in place at Exchange. The Ivatt 2-6-0 Class 3F No **46484,** a series introduced in 1946, is standing on the line used by locomotives waiting to provide banking assistance when required.
R.Keeley

Victoria Station, 19th July 1957. Midland Compound No **41100** on the 9.05am train to Wakefield leaving platform 8. This train ran via Rochdale and Huddersfield, stopping at most stations. No **41100** was, at this time, based at Leeds Holbeck (55A), being eventually withdrawn in 1959. The Compound would have to face the gradient up to Miles Platting, but with only four coaches of non corridor stock it would be no great problem, especially since it was one of a class of locomotives that were used to tackling gradients on lines like those in the Hope Valley and Derbyshire Dales area. *R.Keeley*

(Below) Victoria Station, 3rd April 1959. The length of the freight train descending the incline from Miles Platting clearly underlines how steep it is. The engine, one of those old London & North Western style stalwarts, is 0-8-0 Class G2a 7F No **49119** which at the time was allocated to Patricroft (26F). The train is probably a transfer freight between Ardwick and Ordsall Lane yards.

R.Keeley

Stockport Edgeley, 2nd May 1959. Fowler 2-6-4T No **42357** of Edgeley shed (9B) is seen preparing to move the 5.13pm to Oldham Clegg Street on the last day of operation of the route from Edgeley to Oldham, a route and destination with many cherished memories for myself and, no doubt, many other rail enthusiasts. No **42357** was withdrawn from Edgeley shed in March 1963 and scrapped at Derby works in August of that year. *R.Keeley*

continued from page 10 .... in the Victorian/Edwardian period, referred to the more elegant style of male attire relating to the many formal occasions of the time. So one could say that although the graceful Top Hat has been replaced by a rather shapeless tower of concrete, at least the tails remain, for indeed the station's Victorian elegance can still be observed as soon as one passes through the entrance hall. For it is the classic glass roofing structure, renewed completely in 2000, and columns covering the platform areas that help to bring back the memories. A protective coat and tails as it could be described.

Onward then on to London Road, from the station which at one time carried that name. With a six mile run along an impressive four track stretch that, many years ago, provided me with what I imagined as my own form of Grand National racing event and available almost on a daily basis, as outlined in the pages ahead.

The finishing point for such a race, Stockport Edgeley, one that involved whirling wheels on steel rails, a shattering exhaust and boundless visual output of energy being, as would be appropriate, provided by a railway station of great renown, one of graceful layout and appearance that can impress the onlooker from whichever platform end you view it from. Fortunately, the station still retains much of its classic London and North Western outline, especially where it concerns the buildings and platform layout. The area being further enhanced by London and North Western signal boxes, though for how much longer?

The station nameboards clearly define it as being Stockport, though for many local rail travellers it is often the name Edgeley that is the first to spring to mind. The reason being, of course, that for just over a century there were two quite differently situated stations in the town centre; each of them with a general appearance and, in the case of Tiviot Dale, a name that seemed to fit their area of location. Indeed, these locations could perhaps even give a hint of the station's importance in terms of the routes on offer.

Standing on the platforms at Edgeley one could always sense the feeling of main line importance as those great names from the past, Duchesses, Scots, Claughtons, George the Fifths, drifted into the spectrum. Lengthy trains with the famous names that provided its link to the West Coast main line, London and the south.

In contrast Tiviot Dale seemed to possess a slightly more rural flavour. The station, displaying an almost rustic charm provided by its shapely and elegant Victorian period buildings, appeared to rest deep and comfortable close to the final ending of two valleys and the meeting point of two rivers, Tame and Goyt, the latter then taking a famous name, Mersey, before flowing east - west through a rock cleavage that forms an interesting layout for the town centre on a shallow valley with fairly steep edges.

Edgeley station, on the south western edge of the town centre, sits gracefully above the southern banking of the river, awaiting to provide its main line status as trains approach from a northerly direction crossing the valley on a great viaduct, the latter being one of the architectural gems of the town, albeit on a massive scale.

Tiviot Dale has long disappeared of course and standing above the tunnel entrance, on the main road known as Lancashire Hill, viewing the site is, for me, quite heartbreaking. Indeed, its loss is increasingly regretted by those of us who have some visions of the future transport wise. But perhaps if .... *continued on page 18*

Stockport Edgeley, 26th April 1958. I paused for a while wondering whether to include this photograph since it did not relate to every day services operating from Edgeley. However, since it portrayed two engines from a favourite class of mine displaying some strength and vigour, I thought it worth including. Midland Compounds indeed, not often seen at Edgeley, Tiviot Dale being the usual station to occasionally see them. The train engine is No **41063** and the pilot No **41100.** They are operating one of those special excursions that were much enjoyed by enthusiasts in those days. *R.Keeley*

Stockport Edgeley, c.1958. Caprotti Class 5 No **44741** is seen standing at the southern end of the platform awaiting the right of way. In the middle roads an unidentifed tank, with safety valves blowing off, is on station pilot duties. *R.Keeley*

Tiviot Dale, 27th December 1957. Another misty sort of day which I suppose can be expected at a late December time of the year. The engine No **76089** is British Railway Standard Class 4 mixed traffic type 2-6-0 introduced in 1953. The train is the 1.30pm Manchester Central to Chinley. *R.Keeley*

Tiviot Dale, 5th October 1958. A dull misty morning. A rather lengthy goods train double headed by two of those powerful Stanier 2-8-0 Class 8F's, introduced in 1935, No's **48720** & **48503.** In the rather murky background can be seen the Alligator Mill and by the signal gantry is the bridge that carried the railway across the River Tame within a few yards of where it joins the River Goyt to become the River Mersey. *R.Keeley*

Tiviot Dale Station, 5th October 1958. A rather dull morning but with a camera to hand one tries to make the most of it. The train is the 11.40am Manchester Central to Chinley. The engine No **40411** being what I would have decribed as a Midland "Simple", being a 1912 rebuild by Fowler of a Johnson 4-4-0 with superheater and piston valves. Under BR the classification was 2P.   *R.Keeley*

continued from page 15 .... you are perched in high places the vision, if indeed it exists, tends to become increasingly dim!

These days, Tiviot Dale and the various lines it could have served would be a boon for a large number of the shoppers who use the town centre and the quite nearby superstores and shops and, of course, the market area. Just imagine new rail or tram services and perhaps several new stations, possibly on lines from as far away as Glossop and New Mills etc., to say nothing of the various lines to the west it once gave access to.

Long after Tiviot Dale had closed, I remember one day when I happened to be in the rail information office at Piccadilly Station. A rather anxious lady in front of me was enquiring about train times and which station in Stockport she would arrive at. The answer from a rather cheerful lady assistant, who possibly was a Stopfordian, 'There's only one station in Stockport love and its named Edgeley', and you couldn't argue with that!

Now back to the simmering racers at the south end of platforms one and two, ready and willing to get on their way.

Soon after leaving Stockport they approach an important junction, which at least does carry the name Edgeley. This now becomes a parting of the ways for the two stalwarts of steam and though the race may be over they still face different but hard and gruelling journeys, indeed they will both be slightly travel stained before they reach their destinations. One, Euston, being a terminus of great renown and character, in a city that plays host to so many far famed railway stations which are all part of this nation's invaluable heritage, the other a terminus of rather more modest proportions

sitting comfortably in the centre of one of Britain's highest towns and one of great beauty, the Spa town of Buxton.

The "Scot" or "Duchess" can now wave its own elegant *Top Hat* as it races south towards the west coast main line, with its long train of luxury carriage stock to form its own graceful *Tails*.

The more workaday appearance, but nevertheless quite formidable chap with his rake of suburban stock, will now curve round in a south easterly direction and brace himself to take the high road, so to speak. The hard labour for the wheels on rails that will soon become apparent, the illusion being provided by some comparatively gentle looking Pennine slopes.

But just before that high ground begins to make its presence felt, there is the interweave, in permanent way terms, which was the result of more recent changes at Hazel Grove, changes that brought a railway from the past back into the future.

After Hazel Grove it is an uphill slog and, in the process, passing through an area that today is quite idyllic, a world of nature with beautiful trees predominating, the latter, to some degree, replacing another and rather different one time tangle of rails and ways and late Nineteenth Century industry. The name Middlewood clearly suits its present day situation!

Onward then until we pass through Disley and a 'top of the hill' in railway terms is cleared, giving views of a valley of breathtaking beauty and mystique, all of which will have me wallowing in what has been described as my purple prose, but that must await the next book.

Ashburys Station, June 1992. The front (below) and rear platform faces of Ashburys, which is the second station from Manchester Piccadilly on what was originally the old Manchester, Sheffield & Lincolnshire main line to Sheffield and beyond. The building was a good example of what might be described as a part of our railway heritage. It was erected in 1855 by James Ashbury who owned the nearby carriage & wagon works, the price being £175.00 - a time of quite different money values compared to the present time. I suppose that it is also unusual in taking the name of a person rather than a local area or district. Sadly, by September 1994, the building was in process of demolition due to the widening of the road that passes under the railway at this point. This was another classic example of a station building being cast aside. Thankfully the station is still in use, although passengers for eastbound services are forced to circumnavigate several flights of stairs of the footbridge that replaced an earlier more convenient subway.   *R.Keeley*

Ashburys Station 18th October 1958. Class A5 No **69806** on the 1.00pm Manchester London Road to Hayfield, arriving at Ashburys Station. Around this time these classic tank engines, survivors of a bygone age of locomotive elegance, could be frequently observed on some of those suburban lines that were all part of an interesting past railway development in the south east Manchester area, Gorton shed usually being their home ground.   *R. Keeley*

Reddish North Station 21st April 1958. A view of one of my all time favourites. Horwich Mogul (Crab) No **42848**. Fortunately the photograph is clear enough to display the shed number, 9A Longsight, a favourite shed of mine going back to the mid 1930's when I could observe locomotive movements from a very useful footbridge, at least the building still remains though now for different operational use. The engine is hauling a permanent way and ballast train. The elegant footbridge still remains in use.   *R.Keeley*

Reddish North Station, 13th September 1958. The engine approaching, though dating from early LMS days, presents a visual indication of Midland style. This establishes to be a stalwart from the age of Fowler., one of those great locomotive CME's who so clearly left their mark, Class 4 No **42374** being Derby built 2-6-4 tank engine dating from 1929. The shed plate 9G would indicate that it would probably have been shedded at Gorton at that time. When off duty it would be resting, as one might say, on the bosom of a one time rival! The train is the 12.10 pm London Road to Macclesfield. *R.Keeley*

Reddish North Station, 21st April 1958. A lengthy goods train headed by one of those stalwarts from a past age of steam, Class 3F No **43638** being an 'old Midland 0-6-0' as I might have described it in the days of my youth, a locomotive class that dates from the early part of the century, the Johnson to Fowler years. The engine did not have long to go before becoming scrap metal since it was withdrawn in 1959. There was once a small goods yard, the area now providing use for private business work. However, the shed building remains which provides a visual memory from the past. *R.Keeley*

The Firework Express

Near Reddish Vale Viaduct, 5th September 1958. It would seem that once I start looking through some of my photographs of the Reddish North station area, I cannot resist the temptation to find reasons to use them. Obviously the rail links with areas that will be described later in this book and the next one provides one good reason. This photograph relates to something Donald Evans mentioned in the first letter he wrote to me a few weeks before his sad death in November 1991. Apparently this train when hauled by a Pom Pom was known as the *Firework Express*. Donald Evans had been Station Master for Higher Poynton and Bollington stations from August 1953 to July 1960. So here we have the photograph of Class J11 No **64440** shortly after leaving Reddish North with the 5.49pm London Road to Macclesfield. Despite a long life, the year it was built being June 1908, a life that included some modifications to the J11's, there was still plenty of life and energy in those ageing bones of steel.   *R.Keeley*

Reddish Vale Viaduct, 5th May 1975. Just one of several graceful viaducts that cross some of the many valley ways around Greater Manchester. Reddish Vale is part of a long sequence of valleys formed by the twist and turn of the River Tame as it makes its way down from the moorland on the eastern edge of the Pennines. The footpaths and river views are a heritage much enjoyed by local people.   *R.Keeley*

Bredbury Junction, 21st December 1958. Midland Compound Class 4P No **41157.** The smoke and steam soaring away as it struggles uphill towards Romiley with the 10.10am Manchester Central to Sheffield. *R.Keeley*

Woodley Junction, c.1959. Class 04/8 No **63794** is just emerging from the Stockport (Tiviot Dale) line with a freight train. The line on the left is to Romiley, a line that is still in regular use for operating the service from Manchester Piccadilly to Rose Hill, a line I now regularly use since it allows so many oportunities for viewing the past, as seen in the minds eye of course. The class 04/8 was one of several variants of the Robinson design, in this case with a Thompson 01 type boiler but retaining original cylinders, frames etc.

R.Keeley

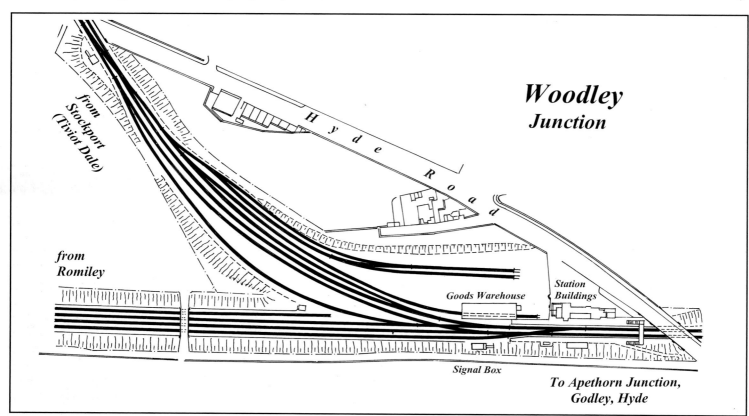

Bredbury Station, 15th June 1974. The train, as I recall, was just empty stock, but the main interest is in the surrounding area since so much has now changed. The remains of the line between Bredbury Junction and leading up towards Romiley is quite visible, as are the twin tunnels seen in the distance and some of the surrounding sidings and industry.

R.Keeley

Bredbury, 14th June 1958. Class A5 No **69817** on the 7.58am Manchester London Road to Marple shortly after leaving Bredbury station, on the approach to the higher of the two Bredbury tunnels.

R.Keeley

.... a racing 'tail'!

Being a nation endowed with a sporting instinct that penetrates deep through the generations, in what might be described as 'the race or the chase' - or perhaps both! Sometimes the affair is of short duration, though for the majority it seems to last a lifetime.

The more popular form of the chase involves taking a large stick (club or bat is usually the preferred description!) and belting the life out of small spherical objects; these are usually coloured red or white! Chasing the ball can also involve a rather larger and, some might consider, less distinguished leather sphere; though such a view could be hotly contested.

With the race we enter a rather different area of activity. Indeed, by stretching the imagination a little, it is possible to see the race as a form of contest involving each of the basic ingredients of this earth - animal, vegetable and mineral.

The animal usually comes two and four legged, and dissimilar forms of the four legged can be seen both in the race and at the chase! The vegetable is the tree grown tall - to spire aloft and make the tall ships. The mineral - metal transformed, two or four wheeled, is often able to make its own form of race track - especially on that motorway lane sometimes misinterpreted as the 'fast one'! But occasionally, four wheels under the right body and with a Malcolm Campbell in the driving seat, can become a legendary Bluebird.

London Road Station, 15th August 1958. *The Comet,* double headed, although I was never sure why. Perhaps the Class 5 4-6-0 was going to be removed at Edgeley or Crewe. However, No **46206** *Princess Marie Louise* clearly displays the elegance of those earlier Stanier Pacifics, though the Class 5 No **44747,** with its caprotti valve gear and lower running plate did, in my opinon, underline a form of mixed traffic appereance.

R.Keeley

Well; although I am not of the sporting type, I did, for a few brief years, find excitement in a race quite different from any of those of more popular acclaim. It proceeded daily in full public view and yet, in the annals of races and racing - and since it could not be categorised among the sport of Kings, was inclined to remain in obscurity: except, that is, to those few of us who, having discovered, thrilled to something that could be viewed as stimulating as anything to be seen at a Brands Hatch or Epsom.

The 'Teatime Handicap' - as it might be described, had all the ingredients that make for an exciting contest. The 'course' consisted of six miles of superbly aligned, almost level and reasonably straight, railway track. The contenders varied from favourites to rank outsiders - theoretically they could even have been considered ill matched, so the odds never seemed too even.

The four track stretch of main line between Manchester's London Road station and Stockport's Edgeley, as they were known in those days; became a race track through one of those quirks in that complex and mystical process known as railway timetabling, which sometimes requires two trains to

London Road, like Central and many other great railway stations, was indeed what I would describe as a Hall and area of Memories. So I thought it might be worthwhile to view a few other classics the station had to offer, there being sufficient of those in the 1950's to arouse our memories of great but now dwindling age of steam power. The magnificent arching canopies of glass were also a means of capturing the magical echoing sounds of steam power, all part of our memories and imagination.

London Road Station, 19th September 1959. Now this is what might be dscribed as the beginning of the end for the *Top Hat*. We most be thankful however that the *Coat & Tails* remain in place to give protective cover over most of the platform areas.   *R.Keeley*

proceed from a terminal station at or about the same time.

The two trains concerned in this race consisted of a humble suburban local and an elite express train of the day; when both trains, for a period in the mid 1950's, departed from London Road for the non stop run to Stockport at 5.50pm.

From the point of view of the enthusiast they were absolutely right for the job, this job, if you like, being to provide the maximum thrill of the chase - especially for the few of us around at that time who were captivated by the sight of steam in full cry. Right for the job too, in the way they represented a contest between a David and Goliath, for nothing refreshes the more optimistic aspects of the human psyche than a trial of strength between the mighty of muscle on the one hand, and the mighty of spirit and determination on the other.

A simultaneous dramatic exit from London Road would underline these attributes; more especially as some of the 'David's' concealed a lithe spring in their step - albeit it was usually hidden beneath a cloak of more laborious working toil.

You can imagine the thrilling, and possibly unexpected sight, as a Mogul and a Duchess blasted in unison the glass end panels of the train shed, in a frenzied tumult of smoke and steam. Unfortunately, it did not always ensure a race, for a simultaneous start could mean that the Horwich Mogul, with its comparatively light load of perhaps five non corridor coaches on the Buxton, would often be leaving *The Comet*, hauling perhaps three times as many heavy corridor coaches, well behind by the time the Longsight complex had been reached.

In the mid 1960's period, and indeed until the end of the decade, I frequently used the 6.50pm to Buxton as far as

my home station which, in those days, was Davenport. The Buxton, during this period, was regularly hauled by one of George Hughes mixed traffic 2-6-0's, his last, and some might consider his best locomotive design; built in his period as C.M.E in the early days of the L.M.S.

The Horwich Moguls, as they were known, were splendid foil for whatever candidate from the big league being used on *The Comet* in those days. They had, at least in my eyes, a jaunty tearaway look, confident and ready to go, challenging the operating authorities to hang anything on their tails. This rather beefy muscular appearance was aided considerably by the rather aggressively inclined cylinders - the boxer, arms and fists up and at the ready, sparring for an opening. No other engine type in the middle league of motive power seemed quite to match this visual image of red blooded strength and vigour - irrespective of thermal efficiency comparisons. Not that I have any reason to doubt their capacity in that direction; certainly there were one or two drivers of my acquaintance who had nothing but praise for them.

In that 1950's period, *The Comet*, which was one of the three principal named trains of the day between London Road and Euston, (the other two being *The Lancastrian* and *The Mancunian*), would variously appear in charge of a reboilered Patriot, a rebuilt Scot, or one of the variants of Stanier's Pacific's. It was the sheer unpredictability that added to the excitement and anticipation.

Hurrying up the long approach to London Road station amidst a host of similarly scurrying figures, (though probably with a difference of intent, for I doubt there were many railway racegoers among them!), one wondered - what will Longsight have provided tonight, will it leave on time, ...*continued on page 32*

London Road, 25th October 1958. A favourite of mine and one of the treasures from the Robinson age displaying its energy and power from almost every angle. Class A5 4-6-2 tank engine No **69806** makes a dramatic exit from platform B with the 12.10pm London Road - Macclesfield.　　　　*R.Keeley*

The Comet

Refreshment Car Express

LONDON (Euston) and MANCHESTER (London Road)

WEEKDAYS

		Mons. to Fris.	Saturdays					Mons. to Fris.	Sats.
			Until 2nd July and from 3rd Sept.	9th July to 27th Aug.					
		am	am	am				pm	pm
London (Euston)	..dep	9 45	9 45	9 35	Manchester (London Road)	..dep		5 50	5 50
		pm	pm	pm	Stockport (Edgeley)	..	.. „	6‡ 3	6‡ 3
Stoke-on-Trent	..arr	12 11	1 2	—	Crewe	..	.. „	6 38	6 38
Macclesfield (Hibel Rd.)	„	12 43	1 34	—	Watford Junction	..	..arr	8§55	9§ 7
Stockport (Edgeley)	.. „	1 2	2 0	1 3	London (Euston)	..	.. „	9 20	9 30
Manchester (London Rd.)	.. „	1 15	2 16	1 12					

‡—Stops only to take up passengers.

§—Stops only to set down passengers

The Comet. A copy of the Comet timetable taken from the Brtish Railways London Midland passenger sevices timetable of the 13th June - 18th September 1955 edition. Interesting to note are the timings on Saturdays when journey times of ten minutes on the Up and over an hour on the Down were longer than during the weekday service.
The Railway Study Centre collection

London Road, 7th June 1957. Another aged beauty, Class C14 No **67447,** is either preparing for a further turn of duty or possibly a return to Gorton Shed. Engines of both Class C13 and C14 had been active performers on local lines from the eastern side of London Road during the 1950's period and thankfully I was fortunate enough to photograph them on many local lines at that time, at locations, some of which, like the engines themselves, are now part of a lost railway world. No **64447** was built in 1907 by Beyer Peacock and withdrawn in December 1958, thus when the photograph was taken the engine was nearing the end of a long life.   *R.Keeley*

London Road, 28th June 1957. Patriot No **45520** *Llandudno* simmers away quietly on platform 1 while wating to move the 8.20am to Birmingham. The engine is what young enthusiasts of my early 1930's days of train spotting would have called a Baby Scot. Understandable since, in overall appearance, they were like a youthful version of the massive Royal Scots built just a few years earlier. The Patriots, as they were officially named, were supposedly rebuilds of the LNWR Claughtons though, in fact, very little of the original engines remained. At the time of the photograph the engine was allocated to 9A Longsight. In those days I was a frequent visitor to Longsight station and to a nearby footbridge that gave railway men access to the engine shed.   *R.Keeley*

London Road, 3rd August 1957. Jubilee Class 4-6-0 No **45587** *Baroda* leaving platform 1 with a southbound express, possibly for Birmingham. The photograph gives a clear view of the signal box provided for the GCR by the LNWR. This was part of the 1900-13 platform extensions and resignalling required by the LNWR as a result of the increase in capacity between Ardwick Junction and London Road, all of which was paid for by the LNWR.

R.Keeley

Mayfield Station, 17th April 1959. This view shows rebuilt Patriot Class No **45530** *Sir Frank Ree* which had just arrived at 1.20pm with the Down *Comet* from Euston. It was during the extensive rebuilding of London Road in the late 1950's and into the 1960's and the dealing with its considerable traffic that Mayfield, being nearby, became a priceless asset by providing facilities for certain services, both departing and arriving. *R.Keeley*

London Road, 8th July 1958. Another view of the Classic, indeed it was my good fortune that there were just a few A5's operating some local trains out of London Road station in the late 1950's. No **69801** is probably awaiting a further turn of duty. In the background, Class J11 No **64310** can be seen shunting vans etc, on the lines leading into the adjacent goods yard.

R.Keeley

Levenshulme Station, 14th August 1958. Royal Scot No **46158** *The Loyal Regiment* hurrying along with the 8.10am London Road to Euston. Tthe station was approximately half way between London Road and Stockport Edgeley. The Levenshulme area was at one time endowed with two stations, the present one being known locally as Levenshulme North, and the other one, Levenshulme South, which has been featured in the first part of this book. The ghosts may remain but only if the imagination stretches itself somewhat. Fortunately the present Levenshulme still offers some excellent local services.

R.Keeley

continued from page 27..... will *The Comet* be a little delayed, or will it have that slight head start that sometimes seemed to inspire the driver of the Mogul with the spirit of contest? So many things to ponder; to sharpen the anticipation of what, in reality, was no more than a routine commuter journey - doubtless to most passengers on the 5.50pm Buxton it was no more than that.

Passing through the ornate booking hall, the traveller entered the station circulating area; it was a kind of transformation - something that could be experienced at most of our great terminal railway stations, the theatre curtain rising to reveal a scenario quite unlike the more discordant one of streets, roads and motor traffic, from which he or she had just escaped; a great-enclosed echoing space pervaded by a vibrant shimmering magical sound. A sound, or since it was in plural, sounds, that might in effect be no more than the subdued fragments of nearby buffered clang or, at the opposite end of the frequency range, the tumult of steam released in mighty roar, each in scale captured by vast canopies of glass and iron, to soar and reverberate in elegant crescendo and thrill those of us who loved these great palaces of steam.

In my imagination, London Road was a hall filled with great music, the orchestral sounds of steam unconsciously creating a unique melodic line that was a joy to discerning ears. The shrill piccolo whistle of that departing Fowler 2-6-4 tank accompanies a balletic pirouette as slipping driving wheels put the twirl on rods and motion. Meanwhile, the hum of deep breathing strings in that quiet andante is really a Class 5 simmering at nearby buffer stops; the sound is stilled yet quietly audible as the fires stir the water within. The distant muffled slow roll of the timpani, reminiscent of the far away rumble of thunder in a Berlioz storm movement, is a Patriot far over against the western wall; now finding respite as, with gentle syncopated exhaust, it follows in the wake of its long train, now being hauled by a smaller fellow towards Longsight Carriage Sheds.

Though the motive power has changed out of all recognition, much of the atmosphere of the place still remains. Indeed, one gives thanks for wise and far seeing decisions, made over a quarter century ago, which ensured the city would be spared the crass horrors that, under the oft misleading cloak of words like 'modernisation' and 'functionalism', made for desecration at Euston and Birmingham New Street, with their dreadful dungeon/ghetto appearance at platform level. The banal inhuman clutter of so much 1960's period architecture certainly has a great deal to answer for!

At London Road, compromise would be the order of the day. The train shed with its splendid curved iron and glass roofs supported by their long legged strides of iron pillars would remain, but the smoke blackened Victorian stone building fronting it, containing the booking halls and other administrative offices, would be demolished. This, in the light of hindsight, was an unfortunate decision; for I have no doubt that the interior could have been modernised while still retaining the outer shell which, cleaned and spruced, would have been a splendid addition to the city's restored Victorian buildings. However, one must be thankful for small mercies; certainly the present combination of old and new is far more acceptable than the concrete snarl that it might have been.

The magnificent train shed may no longer echo to the enchanting sounds of steam though it still captures a more rumbustious less elegant line of diesel chatter. However, if your gaze strays upward, away from the present platform layout, then imagination can also take flight and the old North Eastern platforms, once identified by the letters A, B, and C, are remembered. Great Central/LNER, which used the first three platforms in the station (they approximated in area to the space covered by the present platforms 1 to 5) were separated from the LNWR/LMS platforms (which of course used the numbering system) by a cobbled roadway for vans, and a substantial iron railing, a layout that lasted until the rebuilding of the station in the late 1950's.

Platform A is fondly remembered as the starting point for countless journeys to Sheffield and beyond, behind Sandringhams, Pacifics, Springboks etc.; in the days when storming up the Pennine slopes became an unforgettable experience, especially on the stretch between Dinting and Woodhead. Most memorable of all on that section in the early post war years were the journeys behind the LNER B7's. In the 1946/7 period, these tough looking creatures of steel (J.G.Robinsons ultimate in the mixed traffic 4-6-0 designs for the Great Central Railway) were regularly used on the 5.35 pm out of Manchester Central, a train I occasionally used when visiting friends in Sheffield. The raw blooded vigour of their bark, as they raised the echoes along the shallow snaking curves following the line of reservoirs up Longdendale was unforgettable, shattering the night air of winter that lay in tranquil stillness across the glinting waters.

Even local journeys from platforms B and C could have their moments, especially when riding behind one of Robinson's fiery little 4-4-2 tank engines (LNER Class C13/14) whose vigorous, and sometimes quite stormy departures from London Road, belied their rather elegant Edwardian outlines. Incredible though it may seem, these engines, built half a century earlier, (being one of Robinson's earliest designs for the then relatively new Great Central Railway after he became CME in 1900), were still the mainstay of steam operated local services from the Eastern Region side of London Road until the mid 1950's. Even after their departure for scrap, the Great Central image on these services continued with the formidable looking 4-6-2 tank engines - one of Robinson's later designs (LNER Class A5). They were still operating some rush hour services right into the diesel era!

But all that was a long time ago in a place crowded with bewitching images of steam, a constantly moving parade that would require the bemused platform ender of those days to have pencil and notebook ever at the ready. The variety on both the Eastern and London Midland side of the station was considerable, even in those late days of steam, with engines that came from a dim distant pre group world, to the latest BR Britannia's. Carriage stock also came in what seemed an infinite variety, with a history extending from the beginning to the middle of the century.

Like many of our great railway stations at that time, London Road was a place where the sight and sound of steam was a compensation for decades of smoke and grime that lay encrusted in every crack and crevice, bringing a half light gloom to filter through the glazing.

At night a place of shadows and fancy, the constant background sizzle of steam the glow of fire around the edge of a firebox door - the smells, acrid but aromatic. A half twilight world where a deep sense of adventure accompanied each journey behind steam. With each stride down *.........continued on page 35*

Heaton Chapel Station, 28th March 1959. Patriot Class No **45543** *Home Guard* on the 10.15am from London Road. Known as the *Pines Express* it was a name that dated back to pre-grouping days since it operated along a complex route that, at one time, carried a variety of names of pre-group companies. The express would normally consist of some through carriages with the final destination being Bournemouth West. Thus if you boarded the train at London Road you could find accommodation in a through carriage for that South Coast resort.

R.Keeley

Heaton Chaple Station, 16th May 1959. On a warm sunny day Royal Scot Clas No **46111** *Royal Fusilier* is seen passing through Heaton Chapel station on the fast line with a Up express to London, watched by a small band of those intrepid train spotters, along with the author's wife and son, Kathleen and Michael.

R. Keeley

Stockport Edgeley, 14th August 1959. Royal Scot Class No **46131** *The Royal Warwickshire Regiment* approaching No 2 platform with the 7.45am Manchester London Road - Euston.
R.Keeley

Stockport Edgeley, 17th June 1957. Fowler 2-6-4 Tank No **42397** (shed 9A) is standing on the bay platform line adjacent to platform 3 and is waiting to move the 8.50pm to Oldham. Passengers for Rochdale could change at Oldham Clegg Street and cross to the nearby Central Station for a connection. The 2-6-2 tank engine No **40081** on the bay platform adjacent to platform 4 will be taking out the 8.45pm train to Stalybridge.
R.Keeley

Stockport Edgeley, 17th June 1957. Another view of No **42397** on the 8.50pm to Oldham.   *R.Keeley*

continued from page 32...... a platform the imagination sharpened and came fully alive. By comparison, our present rather blase ease of travel seems to arouse no more than a slight emotional ripple.

However, around 5.40pm at the teatime rush hour, thirty or more years ago, this enthusiast had less fanciful thoughts in mind, as he busily hurried through the booking hall, full of eager anticipation, Scot or Duchess, rebuilt Patriot or a 'Lizzie' which will it be?

Such speculative disjointed thoughts made entrance and exit through my mind on one occasion, I5th August 1958 to be precise, when I hurried along the platform to see what would be gracing the head end of the express.

The disjointed thoughts continued! Why, its double headed, no it can't be , but yes it is, what a turn up for the book. How graceful those first few Stanier Pacific's were, especially in a rear three quarter view, and the pilot, a Class 5, but this one a little out of the ordinary. What a marvellous and unusual combination they made.

As I strode down the platform I was at the same time feverishly opening my briefcase where, since I was attired as a city gent and not a gricer, my old Ensign bellows camera lay concealed. The time was coming up to 5.45pm. departure time for *The Comet* in the 1958 timetable. Sometimes departure did become delayed for a minute or so, but in any case I had to hurry with the photograph then dash over the footbridge to an adjacent platform where the 5.50pm Buxton awaited departure.

I managed to get my shot, hoping that in the haste I had calculated exposure and range with reasonable accuracy; then, an undignified two steps at a time, to arrive, somewhat out of breath, by the first carriage of the Buxton. In the whirl of opening a compartment door and noting our engine, I heard the shrill series of whistles heralding the departure of *The Comet,* and still a minute or so to go before clearance came from our own platform officials, now anxiously viewing last stragglers, while a porter hurried along checking all doors were properly closed. Then, a strident scream from a tiny silvery instrument, and the guard is vigorously waving his green flag towards the driver.

Ah, what a race that might have made in earlier years when the moment of departure for the two trains varied by seconds rather than minutes. Imagine, a Princess Royal and a Class 5 versus a Horwich Mogul, but the express was by now well away towards Ardwick Junction, clearly there would be no fun and games that night.

I stowed the Ensign as surreptitiously as possible into the briefcase, amid the discreet but questioning sideways glances, which the British are so adept at using to mentally query what appears an unusual procedure. Then, in typically British fashion, I slumped in my seat taking refuge behind my newspaper; daydreaming of other days when the starting flags were more closely synchronised and one could start placing bets, even if they were only in the mind, on the outcome.

Out of the daydreaming sprang a recollection of just one of those 'other days', ... *continued on page 42*

Edgeley Station, c.May/June 1959. I was very fortunate to obtain this photograph of what might be termed the number one of Stanier Pacifics, No **46200** *Princess Royal*. The engine is also doing the long turn about and, in the process, passing alongside platform 4 at Edgeley. Unfortunately I either failed to write down the date in my notebook or, since I have a complex of note books dating back to the war years, it has become mislaid. However I have no doubt that the time would be May or June 1959. I certainly could not omit the photograph of such a great engine from the past doing that particular form of reversal.
R.Keeley

Stockport Edgeley Station.

From the early days of railway history, Stockport Edgeley station has always been a most interesting place to view a varied range of train services and locomotives. Of course the scale was even larger when the town possessed that second station, Tiviot Dale. However, there is still much to see, motive power wise, even though the days of steam and also a few of the routes that were an attraction in those days, are long past. So, since the present section is concerned with those later days of steam, I thought I might include a few more photographs to underline that wide range of activity. Especially where it concerns service on routes now long disappeared.

Stockport Edgeley, 3rd August 1959. Fowler 2-6-4 No **42357** (9B Edgeley) is reversing the through carriages which had arrived at platform one from Colne. These would then be joined to the rear of the 10.00am London Road to Euston, after it arrives at platform two. These carriages formed a through service which commenced at Colne at 8.00am. En route they served a number of important towns in Lancashire which included Burnley, Blackburn, Bolton and Manchester Victoria, no doubt a very convenient service to London for passengers from those towns. Perhaps, given a little forward thinking and imagination (if such a phrase is applicable these days) a similar service could still be available. *R.Keeley*

Stockport Edgeley, 29th August 1959. Now a few views at the southern end of the station, the last few yards of platform three being an ideal place for the enthusiast with a camera. Then, camera at the ready, prepare to catch the outburst of steam from all angles as the locomotive of a southbound express, or even a local, gets to grips with its line of carriage stock. In this picture, Stanier Class 5 No **44836** is simmering quietly awaiting the piercing call of a starting whistle. The train being the 4.35pm to Birmingham. The aged companion standing in the bay being a LNW G2 0-8-0 of Bowen Cooke's design, built in 1921, No **49453**. *R.Keeley*

Stockport Edgeley, 2nd August 1957. A view of the Up *Comet* with Princess Coronation Class 8P No **46252** *City of Leicester* simmering in the sun as it awaits the right of road.
R.Keeley

Stockport Edgeley, 24th July 1959. A futher view of the *Comet* with the fireman having a look out of the cab before starting away. Princess Coronation Class 8P No **46245** *City of London* is seen on the Up *Comet* from London Rd. - Euston.
R.Keeley

Stockport Edgeley, 27th August 1959. It is just a matter of seconds before the shriek of a starting whistle announces departure. Certainly the overall appearance of Royal Scot No **46166** *London Rifle Brigade* suggests it is all ready to go, ready indeed to move that long line of carriages forming the 5.50pm. *The Comet*. All part of the enchantment of those days when a great locomotive enhances its lifelike appearance with the varied flurry and hiss of steam as it prepares for the race ahead. *R.Keeley*

Stockport Edgeley, 2nd May 1959. With much leaking steam in evidence Caprotti Class 5MT No **44751** shunts in the carriage sidings at the north end of the station. *R.Keeley*

Stockport Edgeley, 5th May 1959. Late 1958 saw the beginning of the extensive modernisation of London Road station, especialy in terms of the forthcoming electrification and alterations to signalling, track layout etc. One very noticable feature of the old station layout was soon abandoned, this being the locomotive turntable which was large enough to turn Pacifics with their 62' 11" wheelbase. Thus, while steam was still in operation, there was a problem. However, it was soon solved. Perhaps we can look back and wonder if such a similar awkward and unusual situation ever presented itself elsewhere during the period of our steam railway history. So, how to reverse a Pacific? It was achived by running an engine that had arrived at London Road, probably with a Down express from Euston, tender first back to Edgeley station, then along to Edgeley Junction and along the Buxton line to Davenport Junction. (Reversal on to the Khyber line to Cheadle Village Junction would result in another directional change on the Northernden line to allow a return to Edgeley Station.) The engine was now completely reversed. This photograph taken from the north end of platform 4 at Edgeley shows No **46248** *City of Leeds,* having done its turn about, now returning to Longsight shed.   *R.Keeley*

Stockport Edgeley, 16th June 1958. Having viewed a couple of photographs of two of those great names from the world of Stanier, flexing metallic muscle as they begin their race to the south with *The Comet,* I thought it worthy to include a less flamboyant fellow from a similar period making his move. The tender, well filled with coal, giving some indication of the uphill battle that lay ahead for Horwich Mogul Class 5F No **42936** on the 6.02pm Edgeley to Buxton. They were certainly hardworking engines of great character.   *R.Keeley*

Stockport Edgeley, 24th July 1959. One time streamlined Pacific No **46245** *City of London* is gradually coming to terms with moving the 5.58 pm *The Comet.* In a matter of seconds a great spurt of steam exhaust will engulf the remaining curved section of the tunnel, soon to be no more.　　**R.Keeley**

Stockport Edgeley, 29th August 1959. Another view of No **49453** leaving the bay shortly after No **44836** (see page 39) had departed. Since the shed allocation, as indicated on the smoke door, was 9B, one assumes it will be making its way along to Edgley shed just a short distance away. Some engines in this class of 0-8-0's had the addition of a cab fitted to the end of the tender adjacent to the engine cab. No doubt this was a boon in bad weather, especially if travelling in reverse. The photograph also shows the gradual demolishing of the tunnels prior to the electrification of the route, the tunnel on the left being the original double track opening of 1842. The three track tunnel on the right was not completed until 1889, all part of the gradual extension of the rail system and station in the developing decades of the Nineteenth Century.　　**R.Keeley**

continued from page 35...... a memorable occasion when all the ingredients that made for an exciting race seemed to come together.

That particular evening had seen me making unusual haste up the approach to the station, I had been delayed by a business meeting and my main concern was to catch the train. Ironically, in my hurry, I hardly gave a thought to the journey ahead.

No time to pay my respects to the engine on *The Comet,* so identification would have to wait. It was a case of a quick sprint along the platform, amid a welter of whistle blowing to encourage the stragglers, and then just making the front coach of the Buxton; noting that, as usual, there was a Mogul at the front end.

Just two other people in the compartment and the corner seat overlooking the fast lines available - suddenly the adrenaline was flowing. Nail biting seconds as I considered the possibility of a perfect start, to glimpse the carriages of the express slowly gathering speed as they moved alongside the platform edge, with the Buxton ready and impatiently awaiting the starting flag. The express, with perhaps 14 or 15 heavy corridor coaches, really did need a slight head start since, even with a Pacific, acceleration with such a heavy train would be gradual. The Buxton, with a powerful engine, and the acceleration 5' 6" driving wheels would give, could more quickly romp away with only 5 or 6 non-corridor coaches.

I had hardly slumped into my seat and taken breath when I noticed the movement on that other platform. Its happening, *The Comet* is away. The steep rising surge of smoke and steam swiftly erupting, billowing and flowing along the line of carriages as energy evaporated to the heavens, vigour and power visibly unleashed, the long ribbon of the train following a thread in the silvery lined fan of curving rails that form the exit from the station. The Buxton awaits the final starting whistle as the last few carriages of the express are coming towards the platform end.

Finally a piercing metallic shriek answered by the rather more sonorous lusty cry from atop the 2-6-0's boiler and we are away, like the wind. Not every day did steam provide the thrill of such an electrifying exit from the London Midland side of the station.

Lowering the opening window for a few moments and taking a quick look forward revealed the dominating flat side of the Fowler tender. Further ahead a lengthy already rapidly twirling connecting rod seemed intent on whipping itself into ever tighter circles against a flurried backdrop of valve gear, connecting and piston rods, in which each seemed intent in doing their own, diametrically opposed thing, or so the 'cut and thrust' appeared when viewed from the rear.

Perchance the driver possessed a sporting instinct and, since the swaying tail of *The Comet* would now be in his sights, sensed the spirit and excitement of a race; perhaps he only had occasional opportunity to drive what, in effect, was a mini express, for so it became between Manchester and Stockport. In any case there was need for hurry since the Buxton was due to depart from Stockport at 6.02pm, a minute earlier than *The Comet,* and only twelve minutes after leaving London Road station.

So once again, to paraphrase one who also found exhilaration in the chase, the game was afoot, though not it seemed for the other two occupants of the compartment whose heads were now quietly buried between the newspaper folds. Thus none to share, none to coax or silently cheer events which in any case would never see the sporting pages of the daily newspapers.

My own excitement would be contained within; observing the titanic revels of these most extrovert of man made machines in my own private world. The happening may have been shared by one or two others in their own seclusion, a marathon recorded and sublime, but in the mind.

The Comet had a good start, though our own rapid exit from London Road was already beginning to reduce the lead, the tug and vigour of the animal being clearly felt in the compartment. Iron horse, indeed, and how like his flesh and blood brethren, the great dray horses tugging between the shafts of heavily laden wagons that, so recently it seemed, had rolled their iron banded wooden wheels across the cobbled sets of the railway goods depot adjacent to London Road station. By the time the Buxton came alongside the complex of carriage sheds at Longsight, the tail end of the express was clearing the northern end of Longsight station platforms. The Mogul was now tearing along at a deceptively fast rate judging from the energetic sounds coming from the chimney top. The oscillation between tender and cab, and the rapid throw of a connecting rod intent on whipping the relatively small driving wheels round ever faster, gave an almost undignified impression of speed; especially for an engine designated as a mixed traffic unit normally accustomed to moving a heavier less urgent form of freight.

Imagine then, for a moment, a different view, from an end corridor window in the last coach of *The Comet.* Far away to the front, beyond a long trail of smoke and steam, is a great express engine getting well into its stride. To the rear, perhaps a couple or so carriage lengths away, this rather cumbersome looking machine with its little trail of carriages, its smokebox crouching in a high neck of running plate, and what appears an over large clumsy looking cylinder block set menacingly at a slope. The bustling throw of a driving rod and an upward thrusting piston rod, culminating in that challenging roar from its chimney. Why, it's like a head down charging rhinoceros, does it really think it has a chance against a Scot or a Duchess?

A quick glimpse, as we came through Longsight station on the slightly westward bearing curve, enabled me to just get a glimpse of the far away engine at the head of the express, a Scot or possibly a rebuilt Patriot. The gap was narrowing and by the time we crossed Slade Lane Junction the 2-6-0 was coming abreast the last carriage of the express, which, in a few moments, gradually drifted alongside and into my line of vision.

Now, if you have ever been in this position you will probably recall the rather distinctive sound that follows in the wake of a rapidly moving train. The rear bogie truck of the last carriage, now beside you, seems to rock and boom across each rail joint - with more than an impression that it is about to become disembodied. The whole massive shriek of the train seems compressed into an invisible funnelled vacuum trailing from the blank finality, which is the end of the coach. From the lineside it is gone in a trice, but riding alongside it, however briefly, the ringing echo from many steel wheels on steel rails rivets the attention.

Thoughts were crowding the mind, for here I was witnessing the reverse of the traditionally accepted situation. One had become so used to looking through the carriage window of an express and being aware of a receding procession of slower moving and more humble forms of freight. Now came a member of a respected class of mixed traffic locomotives bent on ringing the

Davenport Junction to Cheadle Junction, 21st October 1973. This photograph shows the remains of the track bed of the line close to the point where it crossed the main line from Edgeley to Crewe. The abutments for the overbridge still remain to this day and they can easily be seen if you are travelling along the line. My photograph was taken from the overbridge that carried Adswood Road across the old railway, but not any more since the bridge has been removed and the road realigned, level with the one time rail level.

R.Keeley

changes, if only for a few brief glorious minutes.

Hurrying through Levenshulme, the platform awnings reached across towards the carriage roofs, capturing and flinging back the clattering pandemonium of sound in an almighty shriek of protest as a trailing shroud of smoke and steam enveloped both trains. Gradually, so gradually, the carriages of the express were gliding past my line of vision, like a film in slow motion, but reversed. You knew they were moving forward at a great rate, yet there was the unreal sensation of them floating backwards.

The intrepid Mogul was gradually closing up on the Scot; then came a crescendo in the roar of carriage wheels and general oscillation as the two trains hurtled through Heaton Chapel station, further emphasising the sensation of high speed.

Imagine, for a few moments, you are a platform observer at this place. First you will notice the distant approach of the two trains as they swing gradually round the slightly curving section a mile away, just south of Levenshulme station. Then, in what seems no more than a few seconds, the streaming exhaust from the Scot explodes through the twin arched over bridge immediately south of Heaton Chapel station, followed abruptly by a similar storm of smoke and steam in turmoil as the 2-6-0 in turn bursts out from under the same bridge.

The pulse quickens at the sight or these two machines straining every sinew as they hurry through the field of view, fast, yet slow enough for every dramatic fragment of movement to erupt across the picture frame of the minds eye. The emotions react, a trace of tears to the eyes, knees turning slightly to jelly, perhaps you have experienced it in the 1980's when the *Duchess, Evening*

Star, or anything shaped Swindon fashion came into the view of your swivelling cine camera, or was captured in an instant through the viewfinder of your SLR.

The power and majesty of the Scot is momentarily emphasised as the engine, in a brief rear three quarter view, swiftly passes under the foot and road bridges. Then immediately, in close up, the view is dominated by the 2-6-0; the power is there but the majesty is replaced by a polka like frolic, the boisterous fury of rapid exhaust, the lunging piston rod and a connecting rod madly see-sawing around at platform level, then it is away under bridges, pacing the Scot in a demonic whirl of activity. All that remains is a flurry of smoke and steam swallowing the last carriage of the Buxton and snatching at the last four or five of the express.

Returning to the edge of my seat on the Buxton, no relaxation on this journey, the question is, will we draw level with the Scot before the inevitable slowing after Heaton Norris Junction? The answer is almost immediate as the massive riveted side of the Scots tender gradually slides past the carriage windows, the huge container of coal and water slightly dipping and jolting as six fixed wheels cross the rail joints. There is a momentary glimpse of the fireman attending an incandescent fiery hell, so effectively contained and concealed by the irregular shaped firebox, gripped vice like, or so it seems, by the long running plate, this, likewise, providing a comfortable bed for the long cylindrical container that we call the boiler, a rather prosaic description for the seething cauldron of high temperature water creating the immense power of super heat, which is now as swiftly erupting to the sky above at one end as it is being generated at the other. Surely no other man made machine

Edgeley Junction, 23rd August 1958. Royal Scot No **46160** *Queen Victoria's Rifleman* is captured in the picture. The train is, of course, the 5.58pm ex Edgeley *The Comet.* The flurry of steam more or less obliterates a view of Edgeley Shed and, on the right of the photograph, the beginning of the Buxton branch. At least part of the old goods yards can be seen.

R.Keeley

could give such a close up awesome view of energy unleashed

Now the speeds of both trains is being eased as they hurry across Heaton Norris Junction and onto the viaduct, the carriages doing a reversed glide alongside each other as the Buxton slows for a signal at caution. Reaching the far end of the lengthy viaduct the trains jerkily peel away from each other, *The Comet* to hug the edge of platform two while the Mogul fusses round the curve of platform one.

For a few moments the furore is still, the 2-6-0 sizzles a little as the clamour is transferred to the platform in the form of rapidly moving feet and hurried slamming of doors. Then an urgent shriek from the whistle held by the platform official, imploring, impelling those hurrying feet to move a little faster.

A great gasp of sound hurtles across from the direction of platform two and beats against the eardrums - a released safety valve showing that the Scot is ready for the leap forward.

But the Buxton has the starting flag, the extra moments needed to get long distance passengers aboard the express sees the Mogul first away and blasting through the short tunnels immediately south of the station platforms. On emerging there is approximately a quarter mile to Edgeley Junction. A brief glance through the window as we pass the shed and begin to veer south east towards the Buxton branch, shows a column of vapour white rising vertically above the tunnel exits as the Scot, in turn, blasts away and begins the lengthy feat of endurance for its fireman and driver.

The racing is all over for one day, and if there were no outright winners, well who cares, such end products as scoreboards and winning posts matter nothing, thus did it transcend the sport of Kings and Commoners. For this is the excitement of a race and a chase that scorns the discordant speculation of a gambling stake. What really matters is the sheer choreography of a non-belligerent gladiatorial contest, thus shorn of raging disappointment only the exhilaration can remain!

Table 31—continued **LIVERPOOL and MANCHESTER to LONDON** (timetable)

Edgeley Junction, 20th June 1959. Royal Scot No **46160** *Queen Victoria's Rifleman* gradually getting under-way with the 5.58pm from Edgeley, with *The Comet*. The branch line to Buxton from Edgeley Junction would, in the photograph, be just to the rear of coaches four and five. *R.Keeley*

Edgeley Junction, August 3rd 1957. Horwich Mogul No **42858** on the 8.26am Davenport to London Road station, 7.50am from Buxton. This photograph giving a slightly distant view of the intracacy of the line that formed the junction. The roof top of what is the most southerly of those four most treasured LNWR boxes can be seen to the left of the engine. *R.Keeley*

Edgeley Junction, 22nd February 1958. To be precise, Horwich Mogul No **42923** is just curving away from the junction with the 6.02pm Edgeley - Buxton. The building in the picture was a part of the one time warehouse buildings complex of the Stockport Co-operative Society. That particular building, the Bakery Warehouse, is now demolished.   *R.Keeley*

Edgeley Junction, 18th March 1959. This photograph is included because it makes an interesting contrast to the previous one. The train is the 7.50am Buxton to London Road station approaching the junction. It stopped at all stations on the branch except Dove Holes, Furness Vale and New Mills (Newtown). You usually expected a Horwich Mogul or a 2-6-4 tank engine on most trains on the branch, so it was my good fortune to have a camera to hand to photograph a Jubilee Class No **45560** *Prince Edward Island*. We get an opposite view of the same bridge seen in the previous photograph. It is known locally as 'Bakery Bridge' and relates to the large building also seen in the previous photograph. The tall chimney, with the leters S.C.S., (Stockport Co-operative Society), was demolished some years ago.   *R.Keeley*

Edgeley Junction, 18th March 1959. Almost a repeat of the previous photograph, same train, same engine, but nearer the junction. The train had just passed under Bakery Bridge and still on the curve, so it gives some idea of how lengthy it is, a curve of perhaps 400 to 500 yards before it eventually begins to come to terms with the complex arrangements of points and line crossings as it passes beyond the junction. *R.Keeley*

Davenport, 14th August 1959. The 5.50pm Manchester London Road to Buxton approaching Davenport station. The Stanier 2-8-0 8F No **48680** is not perhaps a class of locomotive one would normally expect to find on a local passenger train on the line, but it did happen occasionally. At least it would provide a form of hauling power that could easily cope with the two lengthy gradients that have to be faced before arriving at Buxton station. *R.Keeley*

Davenport Station, 16th May 1959. The engine at the head of this lengthy goods train is what might be described as a Stanier Mogul 2-6-0 No **42977**, a class that was introduced in 1933. They may not have had the same formidable and powerful appearance as the Horwich Moguls, though in fact there was little difference in the tractive effort between each class of engine. Presumably it will be making its way up to the Buxton area and will probably need much of the mass of coal, which appears to tower up to the cab roof level, in particular to help tackle the two massive gradients it will be faced with.   *R.Keeley*

Davenport Station, 16th May 1959. The lengthy goods train, with No **42977** at the front end, is being banked by a rather heavier looking goods locomotive from a slightly later period. This is WD Class 2-8-0 No **90642**, one of the Ministry of Supply 'Austerity' locomotives that were introduced in 1943.   *R.Keeley*